FARRAR
STRAUS
GIROUX

CREDITING POETRY

CREDITING

POETRY

THE NOBEL LECTURE

SEAMUS

HEANEY

FARRAR STRAUS GIROUX

NEW YORK

Library of Congress Cataloging-in-Publication Data
Heaney, Seamus.
Crediting poetry : the Nobel lecture / Seamus Heaney.—1st ed.
p.   cm.
1. Heaney, Seamus—Aesthetics.
2. Poetry—Authorship.   3. Poetry.
I. Title.
PR6058.E2C74   1996   809.1—dc20   96-48   CIP

Second printing, 1996

CREDITING POETRY

When I first encountered the name of the city of Stockholm, I little thought that I would ever visit it, never mind end up being welcomed to it as a guest of the Swedish Academy and the Nobel Foundation. At that particular time, such an outcome was not just beyond expectation: it was simply beyond conception. In the nineteen-forties, when I was the eldest child of an ever-growing family in rural County Derry, we crowded together in the three rooms of a traditional thatched farmstead and lived a kind of den life which was more or less emotionally and intellectually proofed against the outside world. It was an intimate, physical, creaturely existence in which the night sounds of the horse in the stable beyond one bedroom wall mingled with the sounds of adult conversation from the kitchen beyond the other. We took in everything that was going on, of course—rain in the trees, mice on the ceiling, a steam train rumbling along the railway line one field back from the house—but we took it in as if we were in the doze of hibernation. Ahistorical, pre-sexual, in suspension between the archaic and the modern, we were as susceptible and impressionable as the drinking water that stood in a bucket in our scullery:

every time a passing train made the earth shake, the surface of that water used to ripple delicately, concentrically, and in utter silence.

But it was not only the earth that shook for us: the air around and above us was alive and signalling as well. When a wind stirred in the beeches, it also stirred an aerial wire attached to the topmost branch of the chestnut tree. Down it swept, in through a hole bored in the corner of the kitchen window, right on into the innards of our wireless set, where a little pandemonium of burbles and squeaks would suddenly give way to the voice of a BBC newsreader speaking out of the unexpected like a *deus ex machina*. And that voice too we could hear in our bedroom, transmitting from beyond and behind the voices of the adults in the kitchen; just as we could often hear, behind and beyond every voice, the frantic, piercing signalling of Morse code.

We could pick up the names of neighbours being spoken in the local accents of our parents, and in the resonant English tones of the newsreader the names of bombers and of cities bombed, of war fronts and army divisions, the numbers of planes lost and of prisoners taken, of casualties suffered and advances made; and always, of course, we would pick up too those other, solemn, and oddly bracing words "the enemy" and "the allies." But even so, none of the news of these world spasms entered me as terror. If there was something ominous in the

newscaster's tones, there was some-
thing torpid about our understanding
of what was at stake; and if there was
something culpable about such politi-
cal ignorance in that time and place,
there was something positive about the
security I inhabited as a result of it.

The wartime, in other words, was
pre-reflective time for me. Pre-literate
too. Pre-historical in its way. Then as
the years went on and my listening be-
came more deliberate, I would climb
up on an arm of our big sofa to get my
ear closer to the wireless speaker. But
it was still not the news that interested
me; what I was after was the thrill of
story, such as a detective serial about
a British special agent called Dick Bar-
ton or perhaps a radio adaptation of
one of Captain W. E. Johns's adven-

ture tales about an RAF flying ace
called Biggles. Now that the other chil-
dren were older and there was so much
going on in the kitchen, I had to get
close to the actual radio set in order to
concentrate my hearing, and in that
intent proximity to the dial I grew
familiar with the names of foreign sta-
tions, with Leipzig and Oslo and Stutt-
gart and Warsaw and, of course, with
Stockholm.

I also got used to hearing short
bursts of foreign languages as the dial
hand swept round from BBC to Ra-
dio Eireann, from the intonations of
London to those of Dublin, and even
though I did not understand what was
being said in those first encounters
with the gutturals and sibilants of Eu-
ropean speech, I had already begun a

journey into the wideness of the world. This in turn became a journey into the wideness of language, a journey where each point of arrival—whether in one's poetry or one's life—turned out to be a stepping-stone rather than a destination, and it is that journey which has brought me now to this honoured spot. And yet the platform here feels more like a space station than a stepping-stone, so that is why, for once in my life, I am permitting myself the luxury of walking on air.

■

I credit poetry for making this space walk possible. I credit it immediately because of a line I wrote fairly recently encouraging myself (and whoever else might be listening) to "walk on air against your better judgement." But I credit it ultimately because poetry can make an order as true to the impact of external reality and as sensitive to the inner laws of the poet's being as the ripples that rippled in and rippled out across the water in that scullery bucket fifty years ago. An order where we can at last grow up to that which we stored up as we grew. An order which satisfies all that is appetitive in the intelligence and prehensile in the affections. I credit poetry, in other words, both for being itself and for being a help, for making possible a fluid and restorative relationship between the mind's centre and its circumference, between the child gazing at the word "Stockholm" on the face of the radio dial and the man facing the faces that he meets in

Stockholm at this most privileged mo-
ment. I credit it because credit is due
to it, in our time and in all time, for
its truth to life, in every sense of that
phrase.

．

To begin with, I wanted that truth to
life to possess a concrete reliability,
and rejoiced most when the poem
seemed most direct, an up-front rep-
resentation of the world it stood in for
or stood up for or stood its ground
against. Even as a schoolboy, I loved
John Keats's ode "To Autumn" for
being an ark of the covenant between
language and sensation; as an adoles-
cent, I loved Gerard Manley Hopkins
for the intensity of his exclamations
which were also equations for a rap-

ture and an ache I didn't fully know I knew until I read him; I loved Robert Frost for his farmer's accuracy and his wily down-to-earthness; and Chaucer too for much the same reasons. Later on I would find a different kind of accuracy, a moral down-to-earthness to which I responded deeply and always will, in the war poetry of Wilfred Owen, a poetry where a New Testament sensibility suffers and absorbs the shock of the new century's barbarism. Then later again, in the pure consequence of Elizabeth Bishop's style, in the sheer obduracy of Robert Lowell's, and in the bareface confrontation of Patrick Kavanagh's, I encountered further reasons for believing in poetry's ability—and responsibility—to say what happens, to "pity the planet," to be "not concerned with Poetry."

This temperamental disposition towards an art that was earnest and devoted to things as they are was corroborated by the experience of having been born and brought up in Northern Ireland and of having lived with that place even though I have lived out of it for the past quarter of a century. No place in the world prides itself more on its vigilance and realism, no place considers itself more qualified to censure any flourish of rhetoric or extravagance of aspiration. So, partly as a result of having internalized these attitudes through growing up with them, and partly as a result of growing a skin to protect myself against them, I went for years half avoiding and half resisting the opulence and extensiveness of poets as different as Wallace Stevens and Rainer Maria Rilke; crediting insufficiently the crystalline inwardness of Emily Dickinson, all those forked lightnings and fissures of association; and missing the visionary strangeness of Eliot. And these more or less costive attitudes were fortified by a refusal to grant the poet any more license than any other citizen; and they were further induced by having to conduct oneself as a poet in a situation of ongoing political violence and public expectation. A public expectation, it has to be said, not of poetry as such but of political positions variously approvable by mutually disapproving groups.

In such circumstances, the mind still longs to repose in what Samuel Johnson once called with superb confidence "the stability of truth," even as it recognizes the destabilizing nature of its own operations and enquiries. Without needing to be theoretically instructed, consciousness quickly realizes that it is the site of variously contending discourses. The child in the bedroom listening simultaneously to the domestic idiom of his Irish home and the official idioms of the British broadcaster while picking up from behind both the signals of some other distress—that child was already being schooled for the complexities of his adult predicament, a future where he would have to adjudicate between promptings variously ethical, aesthetical, moral, political, metrical, sceptical, cultural, topical, typical, post-colonial, and, taken all together, simply impossible. So it was that I found myself in the mid-nineteen-seventies in another small house, this time in County Wicklow, south of Dublin, with a young family of my own and a slightly less imposing radio set, listening to the rain in the trees and to the news of bombings closer to home—not only those by the Provisional IRA in Belfast but equally atrocious assaults in Dublin by loyalist paramilitaries from the North: feeling puny in my predicaments as I read about the tragic logic of Osip Mandelstam's fate in the thirties, feeling challenged yet steadfast in my non-combatant status when I heard, for example, that one particularly sweet-natured school friend had been interned without trial because he was suspected of having been involved in a political killing. What I was longing for was not quite stability but an active escape from the quicksand of relativism, a way of crediting poetry without anxiety or apology. In a poem called "Exposure" I wrote then:

If I could come on meteorite!
Instead I walk through damp leaves,
Husks, the spent flukes of autumn,

Imagining a hero
On some muddy compound,
His gift like a slingstone
Whirled for the desperate.

How did I end up like this?
I often think of my friends'
Beautiful prismatic counselling
And the anvil brains of some who hate me

As I sit weighing and weighing
My responsible *tristia*.
For what? For the ear? For the people?
For what is said behind-backs?

Rain comes down through the alders,
Its low conducive voices
Mutter about let-downs and erosions
And yet each drop recalls

The diamond absolutes.
I am neither internee nor informer;
An inner émigré, grown long-haired
And thoughtful; a wood-kerne

Escaped from the massacre

Taking protective colouring

From bole and bark, feeling

Every wind that blows;

Who, blowing up these sparks

For their meagre heat, have missed

The once-in-a-lifetime portent,

The comet's pulsing rose.

[*from* NORTH, *1975*]

In one of the poems best known to students in my generation, a poem which could be said to have taken the nutrients of the symbolist movement and made them available in capsule form, the American poet Archibald MacLeish affirmed that "A poem

should be equal to: / Not true." As a
defiant statement of poetry's gift for
telling truth but telling it slant, this is
both cogent and corrective. Yet there
are times when a deeper need enters,
when we want the poem to be not only
pleasurably right but compellingly
wise, not only a surprising variation
played upon the world but a re-
tuning of the world itself. We want the
surprise to be transitive, like the im-
patient thump which unexpectedly re-
stores the picture to the television set,
or the electric shock which sets the fi-
brillating heart back to its proper
rhythm. We want what the woman
wanted in the prison queue in Lenin-
grad, as she stood there blue with cold
and whispering for fear, enduring the
terror of Stalin's regime and asking the

poet Anna Akhmatova if she could de-
scribe it all, if her art could be equal
to it. And this is the want I too was
experiencing in those far more pro-
tected circumstances in County Wick-
low when I wrote the lines I have just
quoted, a need for poetry that would
merit the definition of it I gave a few
moments ago, as an order "true to the
impact of external reality and . . . sen-
sitive to the inner laws of the poet's
being."

.

The external reality and inner dy-
namic of happenings in Northern Ire-
land between 1968 and 1974 were
symptomatic of change, violent change
admittedly, but change nevertheless,
and for the minority living there

change had been long overdue. It should have come early, as the result of the ferment of protest on the streets in the late sixties, but that was not to be, and the eggs of danger which were always incubating got hatched out very quickly. While the Christian moralist in oneself was impelled to deplore the atrocious nature of the IRA's campaign of bombings and killings, and the "mere Irish" in oneself was appalled by the ruthlessness of the British Army on occasions like Bloody Sunday in Derry in 1972, the minority citizen in oneself, the one who had grown up conscious that his group was distrusted and discriminated against in all kinds of official and unofficial ways—this citizen's perception was at one with the poetic truth of the situation in recognizing that if life in Northern Ireland was ever really to flourish, change had to take place. But that citizen's perception was also at one with the truth in recognizing that the very brutality of the means by which the IRA was pursuing change was destructive of the trust upon which new possibilities would have to be based.

Nevertheless, until the British government caved in to the strong-arm tactics of the Ulster loyalist workers after the Sunningdale Conference in 1974, a well-disposed mind could still hope to make sense of the circumstances, to balance what was promising with what was destructive and do what W. B. Yeats had tried to do half a century before, namely, "to hold in a single thought reality and justice." After 1974, however, for the twenty long years between then and the cease-fires of August 1994, such a hope proved impossible. The violence from below was then productive of nothing but a retaliatory violence from above, the dream of justice became subsumed into the callousness of reality, and people settled in to a quarter century of life waste and spirit waste, of hardening attitudes and narrowing possibilities that were the natural result of politi-cal solidarity, traumatic suffering, and sheer emotional self-protectiveness.

■

One of the most harrowing moments in the whole history of the harrowing of the heart in Northern Ireland came

when a minibus full of workers be-
ing driven home one January evening
in 1976 was held up by armed and
masked men and the occupants of the
van ordered at gunpoint to line up
at the side of the road. Then one of
the masked executioners said to them,
"Any Catholics among you, step out
here." As it happened, this particular
group, with one exception, were all
Protestants, so the presumption must
have been that the masked men were
Protestant paramilitaries about to
carry out a tit-for-tat sectarian killing
of the Catholic as the odd man out, the
one who would have been presumed to
be in sympathy with the IRA and all
its actions. It was a terrible moment
for him, caught between dread and
witness, but he did make a motion to

step forward. Then, the story goes, in that split second of decision, and in the relative cover of the winter evening darkness, he felt the hand of the Protestant worker next to him take his hand and squeeze it in a signal that said no, don't move, we'll not betray you, nobody need know what faith or party you belong to. All in vain, however, for the man stepped out of the line; but instead of finding a gun at his temple, he was pushed away as the gunmen opened fire on those remaining in the line, for these were not Protestant terrorists but members, presumably, of the Provisional IRA.

■

It is difficult at times to repress the thought that history is about as instructive as an abattoir; that Tacitus was right and that peace is merely the desolation left behind after the decisive operations of merciless power. I remember, for example, shocking myself with a thought I had about that friend who was imprisoned in the seventies upon suspicion of having been involved with a political murder; I shocked myself by thinking that even if he were guilty, he might still perhaps be helping the future to be born, breaking the repressive forms and liberating new potential in the only way that worked, namely the violent way—which therefore became, by extension, the right way. It was like a moment of exposure to interstellar cold, a reminder of the scary element, both inner and outer, in which human beings must envisage and conduct their

lives. But it was only a moment. The
birth of the future we desire is surely
in the contraction which that terrified
Catholic felt on the roadside when an-
other hand gripped his hand, not in
the gunfire that followed, so absolute
and so desolate, if also so much a part
of the music of what happens.

As writers and readers, as sinners
and citizens, we have developed a re-
alism and an aesthetic sense that make
us wary of crediting the positive note.
The very gunfire braces us and the
atrocious confers a worth upon the ef-
fort which it calls forth to confront it.
We are rightly in awe of the torsions
in the poetry of Paul Celan and rightly
enamoured of the suspiring voice in
Samuel Beckett because these are evi-
dence that art can rise to the occasion

and somehow be the corollary of Ce-
lan's stricken destiny as Holocaust
survivor and Beckett's demure hero-
ism as a member of the French Re-
sistance. Likewise, we are rightly sus-
picious of that which gives too much
consolation in these circumstances; the
very extremity of our late-twentieth-
century knowledge puts much of our
cultural heritage to an extreme test.
Only the very stupid or the very de-
prived can any longer help knowing
that the documents of civilization have
been written in blood and tears, blood
and tears no less real for being very
remote. And when this intellectual pre-
disposition coexists with the actualities
of Ulster and Israel and Bosnia and
Rwanda and a host of other wounded
spots on the face of the earth, the in-

clination is not only not to credit human nature with much constructive potential but not to credit anything too positive in the work of art.

Which is why for years I was bowed to the desk like some monk bowed over his prie-dieu, some dutiful contemplative pivoting his understanding in an attempt to bear his portion of the weight of the world, knowing himself incapable of heroic virtue or redemptive effect, but constrained by his obedience to his rule to repeat the effort and the posture. Blowing up sparks for a meagre heat. Forgetting faith, straining towards good works. Attending insufficiently to the diamond absolutes, among which must be counted the sufficiency of that which is absolutely imagined. Then finally and happily,

and not in obedience to the dolorous
circumstances of my native place but
in despite of them, I straightened up.
I began a few years ago to try to make
space in my reckoning and imagining
for the marvellous as well as for the
murderous. And once again I shall try
to represent the import of that changed
orientation with a story out of Ireland.

.

This is a story about another monk
holding himself up valiantly in the pos-
ture of endurance. It is said that once
upon a time St. Kevin was kneeling
with his arms stretched out in the form
of a cross in Glendalough, a monastic
site not too far from where we lived in
County Wicklow, a place which to this
day is one of the most wooded and

watery retreats in the whole of the country. Anyhow, as Kevin knelt and prayed, a blackbird mistook his outstretched hand for some kind of roost and swooped down upon it, laid a clutch of eggs in it, and proceeded to nest in it as if it were the branch of a tree. Then, overcome with pity and constrained by his faith to love the life in all creatures great and small, Kevin stayed immobile for hours and days and nights and weeks, holding out his hand until the eggs hatched and the fledglings grew wings, true to life if subversive of common sense, at the intersection of natural process and the glimpsed ideal, at one and the same time a signpost and a reminder. Manifesting that order of poetry where we

can at last grow up to that which we
stored up as we grew.

■

St. Kevin's story is, as I say, a story
out of Ireland. But it strikes me that it
could equally well come out of India or
Africa or the Arctic or the Americas.
By which I do not mean merely to con-
sign it to a typology of folktales, or to
dispute its value by questioning its
culture-bound status within a multi-
cultural context. On the contrary, its
trustworthiness and its travelworthi-
ness have to do with its local setting. I
can, of course, imagine its being de-
constructed nowadays as a paradigm
of colonialism, with Kevin figuring as
the benign imperialist (or the mission-

ary in the wake of the imperialist), the one who intervenes and appropriates the indigenous life and interferes with its pristine ecology. And I have to admit that there is indeed an irony that it was such a one who recorded and preserved this instance of the true beauty of the Irish heritage: Kevin's story, after all, appears in the writings of Giraldus Cambrensis, one of the Normans who invaded Ireland in the twelfth century, one whom the Irish-language annalist Geoffrey Keating would call, five hundred years later, "the bull of the herd . . . for writing the false history of Ireland." But even so, I still cannot persuade myself that this manifestation of early Christian civilization should be construed all that simply as a way into whatever is exploitative or barbaric in our history, past and present. The whole conception strikes me, rather, as being another example of the kind of work I saw a few weeks ago in the small museum in Sparta, on the morning before the news of this year's Nobel Prize in Literature was announced.

This was art which sprang from a cult very different from the faith espoused by St. Kevin. Yet in it there was a representation of a roosted bird and an entranced beast and a self-enrapturing man, except that this time the man was Orpheus and the rapture came from music rather than prayer. The work itself was a small carved relief, and I could not help making a sketch of it; but neither could I help copying out the information typed on

the card which accompanied and iden-
tified the exhibit. The image moved me
because of its antiquity and durability,
but the description on the card moved
me also because it gave a name and
credence to that which I see myself as
having been engaged upon for the past
three decades: "Votive panel," the
identification card said, "possibly set
up to Orpheus by local poet. Local
work of the Hellenistic period."

.

Once again, I hope I am not being
sentimental or simply fetishizing—as
we have learned to say—the local. I
wish instead to suggest that images and
stories of the kind I am invoking here
do function as bearers of value. The
century has witnessed the defeat of Na-

zism by force of arms; but the erosion
of the Soviet regimes was caused by,
among other things, the sheer persis-
tence, beneath the imposed ideological
conformity, of cultural values and psy-
chic resistances of the kind that these
stories and images enshrine. Even if we
have learned to be rightly and deeply
fearful of elevating the cultural forms
and conservatisms of any nation into
normative and exclusivist systems,
even if we have terrible proof that
pride in the ethnic and religious heri-
tage can quickly degrade into the fas-
cistic, our vigilance on that score
should not displace our love and trust
in the good of the indigenous per se.
On the contrary, a trust in the staying
power and travelworthiness of such
good should encourage us to credit the

possibility of a world where respect for the validity of every tradition will issue in the creation and maintenance of a salubrious political space. In spite of devastating and repeated acts of massacre, assassination, and extirpation, the huge acts of faith which have marked the new relations between Palestinians and Israelis, Africans and Afrikaners, and the way in which walls have come down in Europe and iron curtains have opened—all this inspires a hope that new possibility can still open up in Ireland as well. The crux of that problem involves an ongoing partition of the island between British and Irish jurisdictions, and an equally persistent partition of the affections in Northern Ireland between the British and Irish heritages; but surely every

dweller in the country must hope that
the governments involved in its gover-
nance can devise institutions which will
allow that partition to become a bit
more like the net on a tennis court,
a demarcation allowing for agile give-
and-take, for encounter and contend-
ing, prefiguring a future where the
vitality that flowed in the beginning
from those bracing words "enemy"
and "allies" might finally derive from
a less binary and altogether less bind-
ing vocabulary.

■

When the poet W. B. Yeats stood on
this platform more than seventy years
ago, Ireland was emerging from the
throes of a traumatic civil war that had
followed fast on the heels of a war of

independence fought against the British. The struggle that ensued had been brief enough; it was over by May 1923, some seven months before Yeats sailed to Stockholm, but it was bloody, savage, and intimate, and for generations to come it would dictate the terms of politics within the twenty-six independent counties of Ireland, that part of the island known first of all as the Irish Free State and then subsequently as the Republic of Ireland.

Yeats barely alluded to the civil war or the war of independence in his Nobel speech. Nobody understood better than he the connection between the construction or destruction of a political order and the founding or foundering of cultural life, but on this occasion he chose to talk instead about the Irish Dramatic Movement. His story was about the creative purpose of that movement and its historic good fortune in having not only his own genius to sponsor it but also the genius of his friends John Millington Synge and Lady Augusta Gregory. He came to Sweden to tell the world that the local work of poets and dramatists had been as important to the transformation of his native place and times as the ambushes of guerrilla armies; and his boast in that elevated prose was essentially the same as the one he would make in verse more than a decade later in his poem "The Municipal Gallery Revisited." There Yeats presents himself amongst the portraits and heroic narrative paintings which celebrate the events and personalities of recent his-

tory, and all of a sudden realizes that
something truly epoch-making has oc-
curred: " 'This is not,' I say, / 'The
dead Ireland of my youth, but an
Ireland / The poets have imagined,
terrible and gay.' " And the poem con-
cludes with two of the most quoted
lines of his entire oeuvre:

> Think where man's glory most begins and
> ends
> And say my glory was I had such friends.

And yet, expansive and thrilling as
these lines are, they are an instance of
poetry flourishing itself rather than
proving itself, they are the poet's lap
of honour, and in this respect if in no
other they resemble what I am doing
in this lecture. In fact, I should also

quote here on my own behalf some other words from the poem: "You that would judge me, do not judge alone / This book or that." Instead, I ask you to do what Yeats asked his audience to do and think of the achievement of Irish poets and dramatists and novelists over the past forty years, among whom I am proud to count great friends. In literary matters, Ezra Pound advised against accepting the opinion of those "who haven't themselves produced notable work," and it is advice I have been privileged to follow, since it is the good opinion of notable workers—and not just those in my own country—that has fortified my endeavour since I began to write in Belfast more than thirty years ago.

Yeats, however, was by no means all

flourish. To the credit of poetry in our century there must surely be entered in any reckoning his two great sequences of poems entitled "Nineteen Hundred and Nineteen" and "Meditations in Time of Civil War," the latter of which contains the famous lyric about the bird's nest at his window, where a starling, or stare, had built in a crevice of the old wall. The poet was living then in a Norman tower which had been very much a part of the military history of the country in earlier times, and as his thoughts turned upon the irony of civilizations being consolidated by violent and powerful conquerors who end up commissioning the artists and the architects, he began to associate the sight of a mother bird feeding its young with the image of the honey-bee, an image deeply lodged in poetic tradition and always suggestive of the ideal of an industrious, harmonious, nurturing commonwealth:

The bees build in the crevices
Of loosening masonry, and there
The mother birds bring grubs and flies.
My wall is loosening; honey-bees,
Come build in the empty house of the stare.

We are closed in, and the key is turned
On our uncertainty; somewhere
A man is killed, or a house burned,
Yet no clear fact to be discerned:
Come build in the empty house of the stare.

A barricade of stone or of wood;
Some fourteen days of civil war;
Last night they trundled down the road

That dead young soldier in his blood:
Come build in the empty house of the stare.

We had fed the heart on fantasies,
The heart's grown brutal from the fare;
More substance in our enmities
Than in our love; O honey-bees,
Come build in the empty house of the stare.

I have heard this poem repeated often, in whole and in part, by people in Ireland over the past twenty-five years, and no wonder, for it is as tender-minded towards life itself as St. Kevin was and as tough-minded about what happens in and to life as Homer. It knows that the massacre will happen again on the roadside, that the workers in the minibus are going to be lined

up and shot down just after quitting
time; but it also credits as a reality the
squeeze of the hand, the actuality of
sympathy and protectiveness between
living creatures. It satisfies the contra-
dictory needs which consciousness ex-
periences at times of extreme crisis, the
need on the one hand for a truth-
telling that will be hard and retribu-
tive, and on the other hand the need
not to harden the mind to a point
where it denies its own yearnings for
sweetness and trust. It is a proof that
poetry can be equal to *and* true at the
same time, an example of that com-
pletely adequate poetry which the
Russian woman sought from Anna
Akhmatova and which William Words-
worth produced at a corresponding

moment of historical crisis and per-
sonal dismay almost exactly two hun-
dred years ago.

■

When the bard Demodocus sings of the
fall of Troy and of the slaughter that
accompanied it, Odysseus weeps, and
Homer says that his tears were like the
tears of a wife on a battlefield weeping
for the death of a fallen husband. His
epic simile continues:

At the sight of the man panting and dying
    there,
she slips down to enfold him, crying out;
then feels the spears, prodding her back and
    shoulders,
and goes bound into slavery and grief.
Piteous weeping wears away her cheeks:

but no more piteous than Odysseus' tears,
cloaked as they were, now, from the
   company.

Even today, three thousand years
later, as we channel-surf over so much
live coverage of contemporary sav-
agery, highly informed but neverthe-
less in danger of growing immune,
familiar to the point of overfamiliarity
with old newsreels of the concentration
camp and the gulag, Homer's image
can still bring us to our senses. The
callousness of those spear shafts on the
woman's back and shoulders survives
time and translation. The image has
that documentary adequacy which an-
swers all that we know about the
intolerable.

But there is another kind of ade-

quacy which is specific to lyric poetry.
This has to do with the "temple inside
our hearing" which the passage of the
poem calls into being. It is an ade-
quacy deriving from what Mandelstam
called "the steadfastness of speech ar-
ticulation," from the resolution and
independence which the entirely real-
ized poem sponsors. It has as much to
do with the energy released by linguis-
tic fission and fusion, with the buoy-
ancy generated by cadence and tone
and rhyme and stanza, as it has to do
with the poem's concerns or the poet's
truthfulness. In fact, in lyric poetry,
truthfulness becomes recognizable as a
ring of truth within the medium itself.
And it is the unappeasable pursuit of
this note, a note tuned to its most ex-

treme in Emily Dickinson and Paul
Celan and orchestrated to its most op-
ulent in John Keats—it is this which
keeps the poet's ear straining to hear
the totally persuasive voice behind all
the other informing voices.

Which is a way of saying that I have
never quite climbed down from the
arm of that sofa. I may have grown
more attentive to the news and more
alive to the world history and world
sorrow behind it. But the thing uttered
by the speaker I strain towards is still
not quite the story of what is going on;
it is more reflexive than that, because
as a poet I am in fact straining towards
a strain, in the sense that the effort is
to repose in the stability conferred by
a musically satisfying order of sounds.

As if the ripple at its widest desired to be verified by a re-formation of itself, to be drawn in and drawn out through its point of origin.

I also strain towards this in the poetry I read. And I find it, for example, in the repetition of that refrain of Yeats's, "Come build in the empty house of the stare," with its tone of supplication, its pivots of strength in the words "build" and "house" and its acknowledgement of dissolution in the word "empty." I find it also in the triangle of forces held in equilibrium by the triple rhyme of "fantasies" and "enmities" and "honey-bees," and in the sheer in-placeness of the whole poem as a given form within the language. Poetic form is both the ship and the anchor. It is at once a buoyancy and a holding, allowing for the simultaneous gratification of whatever is centrifugal and centripetal in mind and body. And it is by such means that Yeats's work does what the necessary poetry always does, which is to touch the base of our sympathetic nature while taking in at the same time the unsympathetic reality of the world to which that nature is constantly exposed. The form of the poem, in other words, is crucial to poetry's power to do the thing which always is and always will be to poetry's credit: the power to persuade that vulnerable part of our consciousness of its rightness in spite of the evidence of wrongness all around it, the power to remind us that we are hunters and gatherers of values, that our very solitudes and distresses are creditable, in so far as they too are an earnest of our veritable human being.